Pumpkin Fever

Written by Charnan Simon
Illustrated by Jan Bryan-Hunt

Children's Press®
A Division of Scholastic Inc.
New York • Toronto • London • Auckland • Sydney
Mexico City • New Delhi • Hong Kong
Danbury, Connecticut

For Tom, Ariel, and Hana, best pumpkin carvers in the universe.
—C. S.

For Roger, Amy, and Bryan.
—J. B.

Reading Consultant

Cecilia Minden-Cupp, PhD
Former Director of the Language and Literacy Program
Harvard Graduate School of Education
Cambridge, Massachusetts

Cover design: The Design Lab
Interior Design: Herman Adler

Library of Congress Cataloging-in-Publication Data

Simon, Charnan.
Pumpkin fever / by Charnan Simon ; illustrated by Jan Bryan-Hunt.
p. cm. — (A rookie reader)
Summary: In simple text that teaches about shapes, Erin and her
parents buy two wonderful, round pumpkins and while she and her father
carve one into a jack-o-lantern, Mom prepares hers a different way.
ISBN-10: 0-531-12086-4 (lib. bdg.)   0-531-12488-6 (pbk.)
ISBN-13: 978-0-531-12086-6 (lib. bdg.)   978-0-531-12488-8 (pbk.)
[1. Pumpkins—Fiction. 2. Jack-o-lanterns—Fiction. 3. Family
life—Fiction. 4. Shape.] I. Bryan-Hunt, Jan, ill. II. Title. III. Series.
PZ7.S6035Pum 2006
[E]—dc22   2006006760

1 2 3 4 5 6 7 8 9 10 R 16 15 14 13 12 11 10 09 08 07   08

Erin's family had pumpkin fever.

They went to a big,
square field . . .

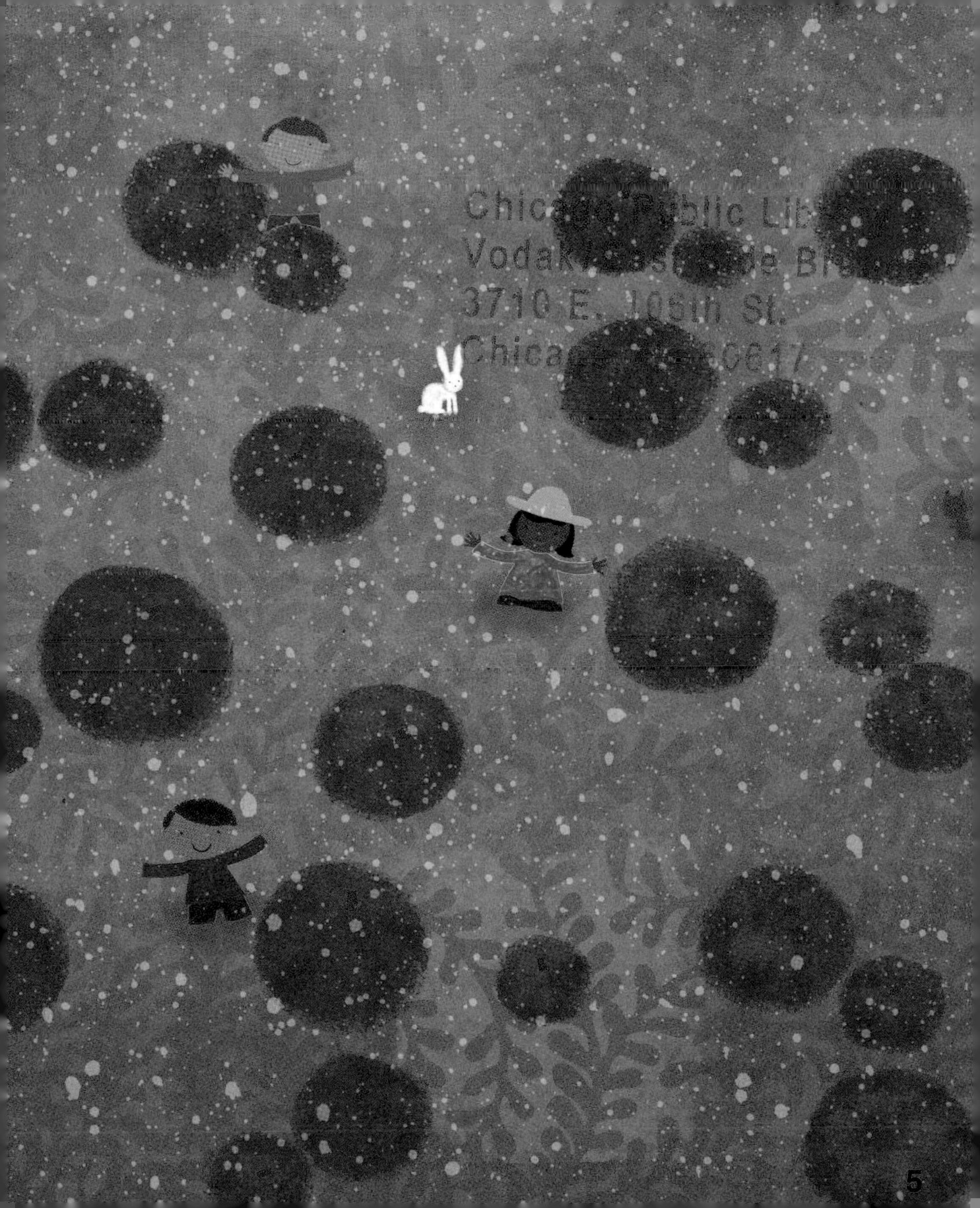

full of fat, round
pumpkins . . .

and chose the roundest pumpkins of all!

Dad helped Erin carve
her pumpkin.

"Two triangle eyes!" said Erin.

12

"Mmm," said Mom. "Very nice!"

"One triangle nose!" said Erin.

"Mmm," said Mom. "I like it!"

"One half-circle mouth full of scary, square teeth!" said Erin.

"Mmm," said Mom. "Scary!"

A rectangle candle made
Erin's pumpkin perfect.

"Mom!" Erin said. "Don't you want a pumpkin like mine?"

"Mmm," said Mom.
"I love your pumpkin!
But my pumpkin is nice, too!"

"Mmm!" said Erin.

Word List (59 words)
(Words in **bold** are shapes or numbers.)

a	Erin's	is	of	the
all	eyes	it	**one**	they
and	family	like	perfect	to
big	fat	love	pumpkin	too
but	fever	made	pumpkins	**triangle**
candle	field	mine	**rectangle**	**two**
carve	full	mmm	**round**	very
chose	had	mom	**roundest**	want
circle	half	mouth	said	went
dad	helped	my	scary	you
don't	her	nice	**square**	your
Erin	I	nose	teeth	

About the Author

Charnan Simon lives in Madison, Wisconsin, where pumpkin fields abound. Her husband and daughters are the carvers in the house, and their pumpkins are sometimes scary, sometimes funny, and always pretty messy.

About the Illustrator

Jan Bryan-Hunt is a freelance illustrator living near Kansas City, Missouri, with her husband and two children. Jan and her family enjoy visiting a local pumpkin patch every fall.